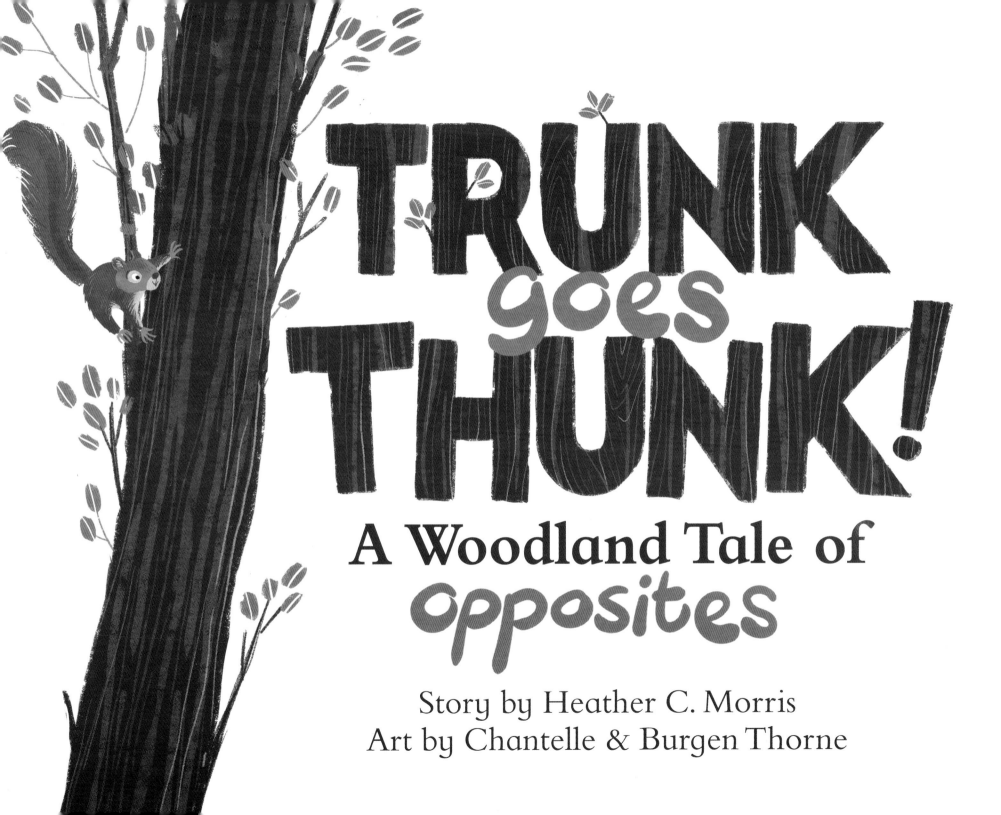

TRUNK goes THUNK!

A Woodland Tale of opposites

Story by Heather C. Morris
Art by Chantelle & Burgen Thorne

GNOME ROAD PUBLISHING
Louisville, Kentucky, USA
www.gnomeroadpublishing.com
Logo designs by Wendy Leach,
Copyright © 2024 by Gnome Road Publishing
Library of Congress Control Number: 2023951507
LC record available at:
https://lccn.loc.gov/2023951507
ISBN 978-1-957655-29-1 (trade)
ISBN 978-1-957655-33-8 (ebook)
Summary: A lyrical nonfiction account of forest
animals repurposing a fallen tree as a log bridge
through the use of playful word opposites.
The text of this book is set in Bembo Infant.
Book design by Chantelle and Burgen Thorne
First Edition
10 9 8 7 6 5 4 3 2 1
Manufactured in China

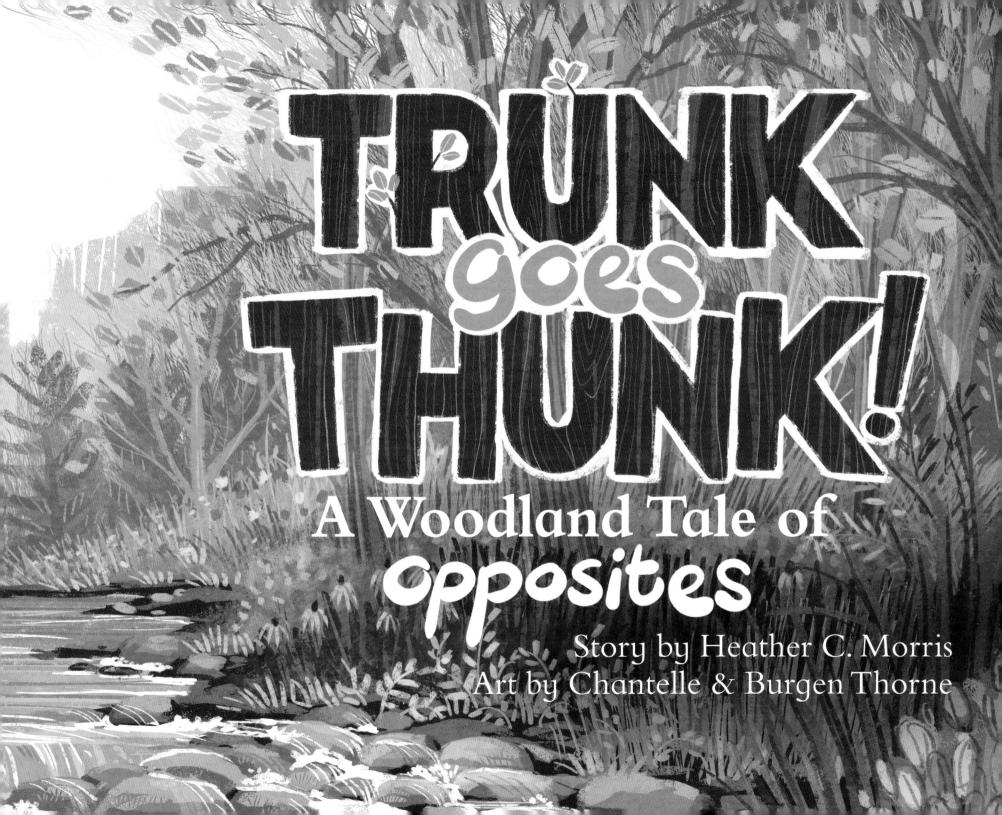

TRUNK goes THUNK!

A Woodland Tale of opposites

Story by Heather C. Morris

Art by Chantelle & Burgen Thorne

Deep in the sun-splashed forest,
all is **quiet**. Then ...
suddenly ... a **loud**

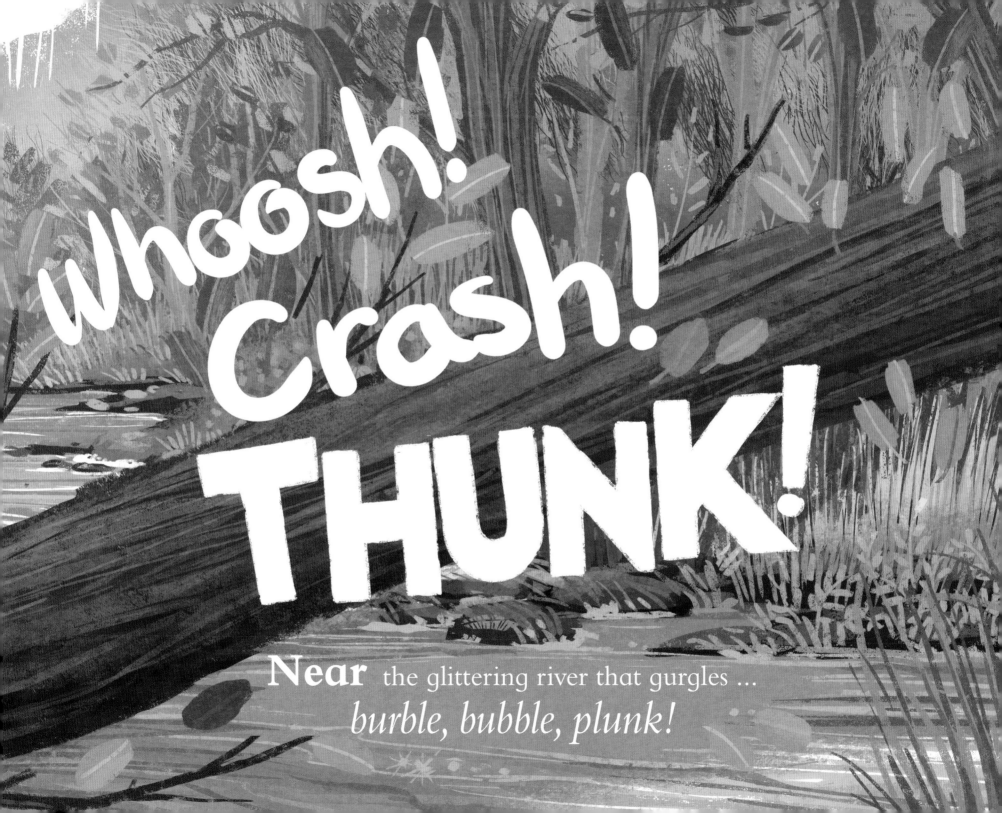

Whoosh! Crash! THUNK!

Near the glittering river that gurgles ...
burble, bubble, plunk!

Far away, forest animals prick their ears.

"*What could it be?*"

They crinkle their noses.

"*Should we go see?*"

Some crawl and creep
on one riverbank.
More hop and leap
on the other.

Separated
by the river,

but all **together**
they find a toppled tree.

It has towered tall
for many **sunrises**.

Many **sunsets**.

Through sticky
summers

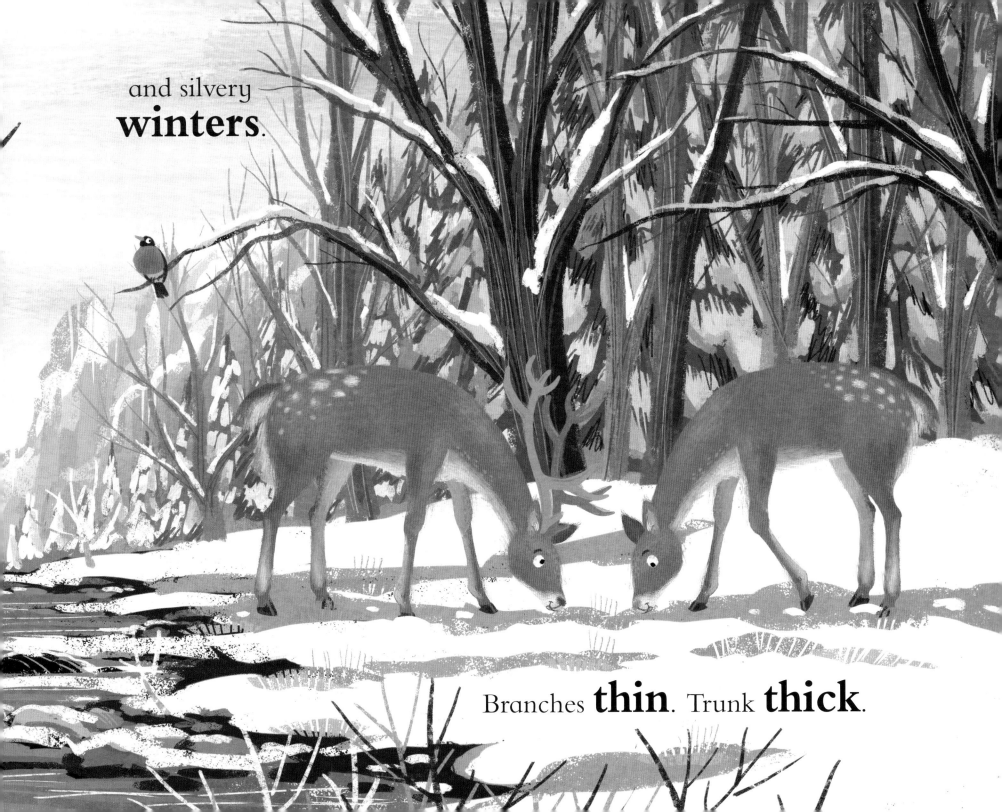

and silvery **winters**.

Branches **thin**. Trunk **thick**.

Day by day,
pawprint by pawprint,

the tumbled tree is
transformed into
a *bridge*.

Just right for a bear to balance,
forward to one side ...

And **back** again.

For ducks to float **under**.

And a fox to run **over**.

For **small** skittering mice.

And **large**
prancing deer.

For **hot** summer sunning.

And **cold** winter wandering.

For raccoons
to travel in the
dark.

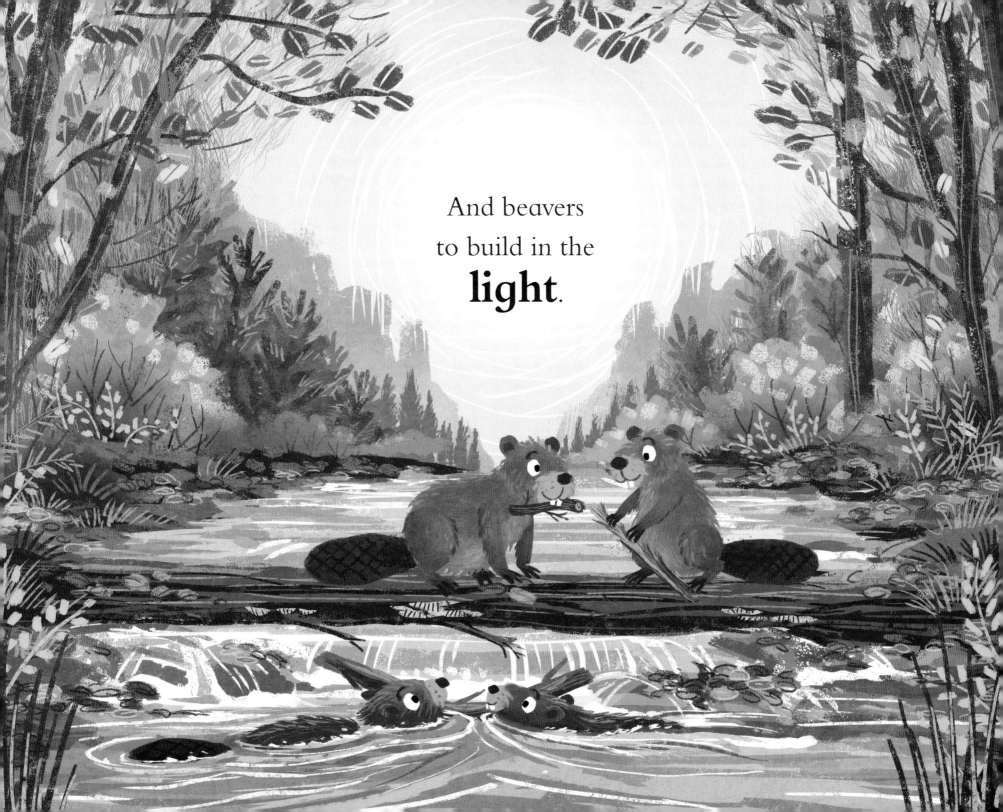

And beavers
to build in the
light.

For eagles
to hunt **high**.

And fish to swim **low**.

For a lynx to dash **fast**.

And a porcupine to amble **slow**.

Forest animals **young** and **old**
trace paths new and bold.

No longer **separated**.
Now **together**.

All because

a trunk went

THUNK!

To Chris, Luke, Clara, and Jenna. You are my **together**.

Heather C. Morris

worked as a scientist for years before she began writing books and stories full of science, wonder, and imagination for kids of all ages. She lives with her husband and their three children in the foothills of the Appalachian Mountains, where they love to hike and look for trunks that have gone THUNK! This is her debut picture book. Visit her online at **heathercmorris.com**.

With appreciation for all things wild and **wonderful**.

Chantelle & Burgen Thorne

are a multi-award-winning (married) illustration team. They live in the countryside surrounded by tall trees and an amazing variety of wild birds and animals. When they're not at their desks illustrating stories for kids, you'll find them being towed around the woodland paths by their beloved dogs. Find them online at **chantelleandburgen.com**.

Head on over to the Gnome Road website for complementary educational resources and coloring sheets. Simply scan this code: